SEPARATED AT BIRTH?

SEPARATED

A SPY BOOK

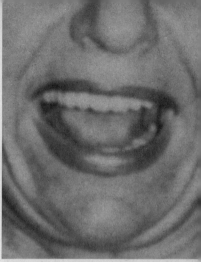

AT BIRTH?

by the Editors of SPY

A Dolphin Book
Doubleday

New York London Toronto Sydney Auckland

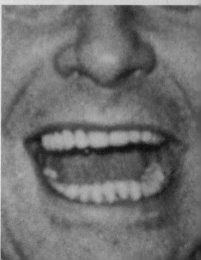

Picture Editor Amy Stark
Design Drenttel Doyle Partners
Associate Picture Editor Julie Mihaly
Picture Research Assistants Susan Buttenwieser
Blake Eskin
Nicki Gostin

A Dolphin Book
Published by Doubleday, a division of
Bantam Doubleday Dell Publishing Group, Inc.
666 Fifth Avenue, New York, New York 10103
Dolphin, Doubleday, and the portrayal of
two dolphins are trademarks of Doubleday, a division of
Bantam Doubleday Dell Publishing Group, Inc.

Library of Congress Cataloging-in-Publication Data
Separated at birth? / by the editors of Spy. — 1st ed.
p.   cm.
"A Dolphin book."
Includes index.
ISBN 0-385-24744-3
1. Look alikes — Humor.   2. Celebrities — Humor.
3. American wit and humor.   I. Spy (New York, N.Y.)
PN6231.L58S47 1988
920′.02 — dc19   88-20213
CIP

The title *Separated at Birth?*™ is a trademark of
SPY PUBLISHING PARTNERS, L.P.

CONTENTS

THE MAKING OF SEPARATED AT BIRTH?

When the initial plans for SPY were drawn up, back between the wars, we set ourselves an ambitious goal. We were determined, with our magazine, to do something absolutely different. Our Vision — let's not be modest, that's what it was — required us to break the mold, go against the grain, dance to a different drummer, and any number of other clichés. That is the way visionaries operate, by the way. • So we looked around at what was being published, and we were, we don't mind telling you, appalled. There was social satire, to be sure, and there were newsweeklies, but nothing *really* important. Nothing that mattered. *America deserves a magazine*, we thought, *that* . . . but then we kind of lost the thread, decided to go out for a bite, and didn't meet again for several weeks. When we did, we knew what we wanted. *America deserves a maga-zine*, we thought, *in which photographs of unrelated people who look alike can be placed side by side to possibly comic effect*. In retrospect, it seems so obvious. Yet at the time, it is important to remember now, this was dangerous, dangerous thinking, and everyone who cared about us said we were reckless, crazy fools. • But did we listen? Well, yes. Our vision clouded, and we basically let the matter drop for half a century — in fact, we let it drop until the third issue of SPY, in December 1986. There, on page eleven (in those days, that meant toward the *back* of the magazine), under the heading "Separated at Birth?," we published photographs of Edward M. Kennedy, the high-spirited Democratic senator, and Sarah Ferguson, the high-spirited democratic duchess; short, wacky war strategist Caspar W. Weinberger and shortish, wacky artiste Jean Cocteau; and Meryl Streep and Mike Nichols. Six little snapshots that, many experts feel, changed the face of American journalism. The fact that there were two cross-sexual pairs out of three in the very first installment was the most obvious tip-off that we wouldn't be going for easy Frank Perdue/Ed Koch pairings. *If this be slapstick*, we reasoned, *make the most of it.* • We live in a very different world now than we did back in late 1986, but "Separated at Birth?" remains a constant, having appeared in every issue of SPY since then. Among the milestones: JANUARY–FEBRUARY 1987. Four pairs are used instead of three, causing murmurs in New York publishing circles. One of the pairs is especially chilling: Vincent Price and Eve Arden. MARCH 1987. SPY's first cross-species "Separated at Birth?" appears: Clint Eastwood and a baboon. This, apparently, is The Issue No One Saw. In it, we also pair the allegedly larcenous Leona Helmsley and the late Liberace, a couple that continues to be recommended to us almost weekly as "perfect for your 'Separated at Birth?' section." APRIL 1987. Secretary of State George Shultz is paired with Bert Lahr's Cowardly Lion, as

SPY introduces the fictional element into the equation. We also publish a letter from a reader who says he hates virtually everything in SPY *except* "Separated at Birth?" We resolve to continue the section anyway. SEPTEMBER 1987. Notable for our second *Wizard of Oz* reference—Oliver North/Wicked Witch's winged monkey—and for the Tama (*Slaves of New York*) Janowitz/Al (Grandpa Munster) Lewis combination. DECEMBER 1987. Bonanza! Tama and Al are reunited—only their 8×10 glossies had met in September—and pose together for the issue's cover. Seven full pages of "Separated at Birth?" are contained within, almost too much fun for ordinary men and women. The extravaganza includes a few new twists, such as "Triplets" and the "Homicidal Maniac Edition." MARCH 1988. Suggestions from readers, already on the increase, reach a crescendo in the wake of the December issue, and we finally deal with it all in our "From the SPY Mailroom" column. Apart from such inspired ideas as George Shultz/Cowardly Lion and, of course, Leona Helmsley/Liberace, people have begun to volunteer friends and relatives as well as celebrities. ("My husband is a dead ringer for President Daniel Ortega," begins a typical letter.) Other readers cite primitive forerunners of SPY's "Separated at Birth?" in England's *Private Eye* magazine and in the old prewar *Vanity Fair*. We acknowledge this and silently blame ourselves for not having gone with our gut feeling when we first had the idea, many, many years ago. We also pay tribute to the imitators *we* have spawned in publications throughout the United States and greater Stockholm. (In those instances where imitators use the federally trademarked name "Separated at Birth?" but fail to credit SPY, we pay tribute by way of our attorneys.) • Through all this, we've never looked back. "Separated at Birth?" remains enormously popular, even among people who also read some of the articles in SPY. "Skimmed that piece on Donald Trump," we would hear, typically. "Very nice. But that William Casey/ Eleanor Roosevelt pairing? *Brilliant*." • People wonder how we do it. • We've tried open calls for look-alikes. (Honest. The guy who thinks he looks like Brando is still calling.) We've tried messing about in laboratories with developing fluid and infrared light.

We've even tried tricking famous people on the street and then snapping their picture. (*Please, Mr. Rather, would you shift your part just for a second, now curl your lip a bit . . . a bit more . . . there! ELVIS! ELVIS! That is ELVIS, as I live and breathe.*) • But we've learned that it's really much simpler than that. Here's the secret: You see, there's this one person, and you notice that he looks like this other person, and then you *get a whole bunch of photos*. Then you pick out the best pair, and run them side by side at the same size, which seems to work better than, say, running them several pages apart or in separate issues, or publishing one at postage-stamp size and the other as a billboard. So, anyway, you run them side by side, and maybe, just maybe, you do what you can to make sure they're facing sort of the same way and have, if possible, similar expressions or gestures. *That's all!* If a few people laugh, you do it again. If a few more people laugh, you expand the joke into a feature. And if enough people laugh, you get a book deal. • People wonder *why* we do it. • We admit that we enjoy creating surprising, incongruous "Separated at Birth?" couples. Well-known people who wouldn't normally be thought of in the same moment suddenly find themselves indelibly joined (in the public's mind), in effect burdened (in the public's mind) by having to prove that not only *don't* they share the same parents but, in all likelihood, they don't have any connection whatsoever with each other—which, of course, they now (in the public's mind) do. So: are we trying to make some sort of *point* by pairing Jim Bakker with Herve Villechaize, Calvin Trillin with Lee Harvey Oswald, Walter Cronkite with Captain Kangaroo, or Alger Hiss with David Leisure? No. We're just in the entertainment business. At least, that's our story. • In this modest volume, SPY, through the modern miracle of "Separated at Birth?," brings hundreds of different people (and animals and cartoon characters) together. All these disparate people—some of them dead, some of them fictional—all meeting on the pages of our little book. *Isn't it beautiful?* This is what keeps us going. From a few little photos to a magazine cover to . . . a book. • We can pretty much promise you there won't be a movie. But *Separated at Birth: The Traveling Slide Presentation*—that, we will never rule out.

—*The Editors of SPY*

Rock and/or Roll

R

hythm & blues, rock 'n' roll, soul, folk,
whatever — it's time to throw those awful
target-audience subdivisions out the window, and maybe
push the radio programmers out after them. It's all *music*, man. And, like,
what could be more, you know, like, *egalitarian* than
Graham Nash leading the NBC Orchestra on *The Tonight Show* or
Don Knotts taking a crack at "Honky Tonk Women."

Briefly interesting politician Geraldine Ferraro . . .   **and intermittently interesting pop star David Bowie?**

Generic sitcom actress
Pam Dawber . . .

and relentless rock singer
Grace Slick?

David "Buster Poindexter"
Johansen . . .

and Princess "Buster
Grimaldi" Stephanie?

Alleged wife-attacker
James Brown . . .

and goblet-breaker
Ella Fitzgerald?

Talented musician
Peter Gabriel . . .

and talentless technocrat
Peter Ueberroth?

Popular-music-
titan-of-his-generation
George Gershwin . . .

and popular-music-
titan-of-his-generation
Bruce Springsteen?

Three Amigos star
Chevy Chase . . .

and overrated-dead-singer-
turned-cottage-industry
Jim Morrison?

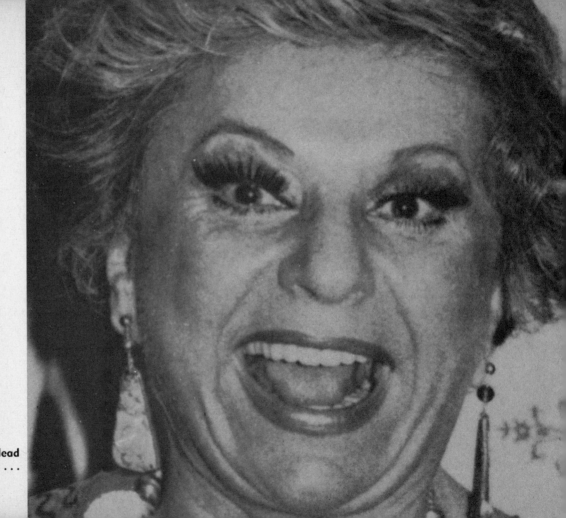

Objectionable dead comedienne Totie Fields . . .

and objectionable live geek
Ozzy Osbourne?

Mick Jagger . . .

and Don Knotts as The Incredible Mr. Limpet?

Charlie Watts . . .

and Buster Keaton?

Ladies and Gentlemen . . . most of the Rolling Stones!

Ron Wood . . .

and *Ed Sullivan Show* fossil Charlie Callas?

Ladies and Gentlemen . . .
one half of U2 . . . that's, uh, U1?

Bono Vox . . .

and insanely inventive
comedian Robin Williams?

Dave "The Edge" Evans . . .

and gabby New York Met
Gary Carter?

Misunderstood recluse
Paul McCartney . . .

and Angela Lansbury?

Hairweave experiment
David Lee Roth . . .

and *Kitten with a Whip* star
Ann-Margret?

Ill-tempered legend
Chuck Berry . . .

and comic genius
Jerry Stiller?

Janis Joplin . . .

and *Facts of Life*'s Mindy Cohn?

Bette Midler . . .

and Dee Snider of Twisted Sister?

Tina Turner . . .

and Edward G. Robinson?

Well-born musician-to-be Sean Lennon . . .

and well-married former actress Merle Oberon?

Grating comedian Emo Philips . . .

and grating folksinger Suzanne Vega?

And finally . . . Nobody, Nobody, Nash, and Young!

Graham Nash . . .

and Doc Severinsen?

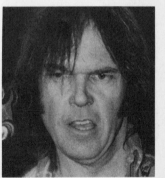

Neil Young . . .

**and fashion designer
Stephen Sprouse?**

Born Again?

**Ancient actor
George C. Scott . . .**

**and Ancient Greek
Epicurus?**

he Shirley MacLaine section.
Confirmation at last for the school of
thought that believes Charles Darwin
didn't become extinct but evolved into
cartoonist Gary Larson.

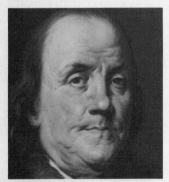

Escape artist
Harry Houdini . . .

and Romantic artist
Jean-Honoré Fragonard?

Abraham Lincoln . . .

and Jean Simmons?

Inventor-statesman-lothario
Benjamin Franklin . . .

and cretin—neighbor—butt-
of-jokes Larry (William
Sanderson) from *Newhart?*

Animal caricaturist
Gary Larson . . .

and animal caricaturist
Charles Darwin?

Suspicious-Similarity-Gate

By election, by
appointment, by marriage,
and . . . by God, we think
we just voted for
Ernest Borgnine!

Charismatic New York toastmaster Mario Cuomo . . .   **and charismatic Lebanese leader Nabi Berri?**

Ex-National Security Adviser Zbigniew Brzezinski . . .

and former National League pitcher Jim Bouton?

Former U.S. Secretary of Labor William Brock . . .

and young Marcello Mastroianni?

Lawmaker John Tower . . .

and cocktail-shaker W. C. Fields?

Former New York Governor Hugh Carey . . .

and former disaster-movie fixture Ernest Borgnine?

Can't Remember Either One Running for President

**Mush-brained politician
Jack Kemp . . .**

**and mush-mouthed actor
Clu Gulager?**

**First Lady wanna-be
Lee Hart . . .**

**and character actor
Tom Poston?**

**Non-Yiddish-speaking
Senator Alan Cranston . . .**

**and *Yentl* author
Isaac Bashevis Singer?**

**Wife-dominated
Senate Minority Leader
Robert Dole . . .**

**and wife-dominated Cuban
bandleader Desi Arnaz?**

Washington-resident postcandidate Bruce Babbitt . . .

and *Washington Post* publisher Katharine Graham?

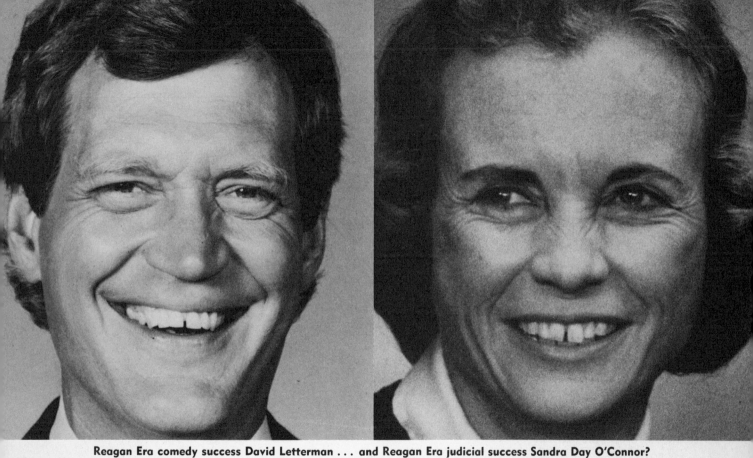

Reagan Era comedy success David Letterman . . . and Reagan Era judicial success Sandra Day O'Connor?

Serene, seemly daughter-of-famous-actress Mia Farrow . . .

and anguished, unseemly daughter-of-famous-politician Amy Carter?

Foul-opinioned jurist Robert Bork . . .

and foul-mouthed comedian Redd Foxx?

**Right-wing nut
Lieutenant General
James Abrahamson . . .**

**and left-wing nut
Vanessa Redgrave as
Renée Richards?**

Michael "Mike" Dukakis . . .

and Fred "Mister" Rogers?

Thoroughly Delightful Pair

**1970s sensation
Martha Mitchell . . .**

**and 1970s sensation
Don Rickles?**

 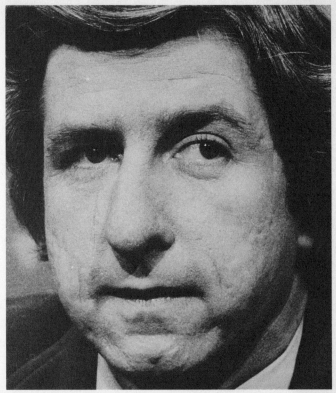

Still-living-abroad-director—child-molester Roman Polanski . . .   and still-just-a-state-legislator—Fonda-husband Tom Hayden?

Decent actor Crispin Glover . . .

and indecent presidential candidate George Bush?

That Whole
Iran-Contra
Unpleasantness

Arms for hostages?
Diverted funds?
Sounds like fodder
for a TV movie.
Here's the preliminary
cast list.

Billy Crystal as . . .

contra leader Pedro Joaquín
Chamorro Cardenal

Treasury Secretary
James Baker as . . .

conspirator—suicide-amateur
Robert McFarlane

Eleanor Roosevelt as . . .

late CIA Director
William Casey

Mrs. Oliver North as . . .

General Richard Secord

Saturday Night Live's
Dennis Miller as . . .

Oliver North

Dan Aykroyd as . . .

congressional witness
William B. O'Boyle

Who in the World?

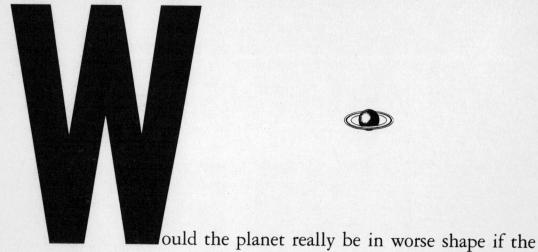

Would the planet really be in worse shape if the people in charge turned out to be Frank Sinatra,

Ann B. Davis, Inspector Clouseau, and Cher?

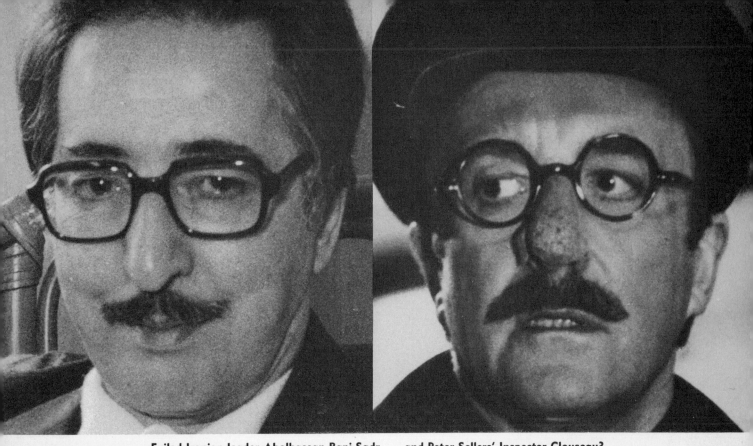

Exiled Iranian leader Abolhassan Bani-Sadr . . . and Peter Sellers' Inspector Clouseau?

Ruthless foreign-born
Argentinian dictator
Eva Perón . . .

and ruthless foreign-born
casino dictator
Ivana Trump?

Pakistan's late President
Mohammad Zia ul-Haq . . .

and *Cagney and Lacey*'s
Sharon Gless?

French leader
François Mitterrand . . .

and actor Robert Duvall?

The royal bunch's
Sarah Ferguson . . .

and *The Brady Bunch*'s
Ann B. Davis?

*I Am
Syrian.
I Enjoy
Syrian
Customs
and Syrian
Foods of
All Kinds*

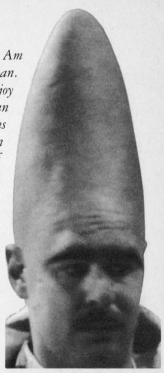

Unrepentant Nazi
Rudolf Hess . . .

and unrelenting advocate
Ralph Nader?

Syria's President
Hafez al-Assad . . .

and *Saturday Night Live*'s
Beldar Conehead?

Anwar "The
Thomas Jefferson of
Egypt" al-Sadat . . .

and Sherman "*The
Jeffersons* of America"
Hemsley?

Difficult former UNESCO chief Amadou Mahtar M'Bow . . .   **and difficult former singing great Frank Sinatra?**

**Sri Lankan president
J. R. Jayewardene . . .**

and wealth accumulator
Bill Cosby?

Apologist for dictators
Jeane Kirkpatrick . . .

and former CIA official
Bobby Ray Inman?

Tiresome would-be Pakistani
leader Benazir Bhutto . . .

and tiresome would-be
serious actress Cher?

Iranian leader Hojatolislam
Ali Khamenei . . .

and Woody Allen?

Washington social expert
Letitia Baldrige . . .

and London anti-socialist
Margaret Thatcher?

Burying the Cold War

East is East,
West is West,
and — yo —
the twain shall meet.

Mikhail "Spot" Gorbachev . . .

**and purged *New Yorker*
editor William "Mr." Shawn?**

Raisa Gorbachev . . .

and Vicki Lawrence?

Mod Communist Angela Davis . . .

and *Mod Squad* actor Clarence Williams III?

**Communist spokesman
Gennadi Gerasimov . . .**

**and anti-Communist
spokesman William Safire?**

**Soviet Foreign Minister
Eduard Shevardnadze . . .**

**and British actor
Nicol Williamson?**

Possible Communist liar Alger Hiss . . .

and popular car-sales liar David "Joe Isuzu" Leisure?

Soviet astronaut Yuri Gagarin . . .

and *Right Stuff* astronaut Ed Harris?

Former Soviet Foreign Minister Andrei Gromyko . . .

and actor Tom Ewell?

Solidarity-crushing Polish leader Wojciech Jaruzelski . . .

and solidarity-crushing New York mayor Ed Koch?

Office of the Chairman

Where there's money,
there's often realistic, hard-to-distinguish counterfeit
money too. In other words, it takes
a sharp eye to keep from sending Martina Navratilova
to prison for insider trading.

**Architect
Robert A. M. Stern . . .**

**and Merck chieftain
Roy Vagelos?**

Billionaire Sid Bass . . .

and actress JoBeth Williams?

**Former greenmailer
Carl Icahn . . .**

**and former comedian
Mel Brooks?**

**1960s-oddity-survivor
Vidal Sassoon . . .**

**and 1960s-oddity-
survivor Orson Bean?**

Profligate, party-throwing publisher Malcolm Forbes . . .   **and prolific, forest-destroying author Isaac Asimov?**

Chrysler's Lee Iacocca . . .

and Carson's Ed McMahon?

**Prison-time-server
Ivan Boesky . . .**

**and powerful tennis-server
Martina Navratilova?**

**Fiat tycoon
Giovanni Agnelli . . .**

**and baseball manager
Sparky Anderson?**

The Three Faces of Elvis

*Queens-born casino operator
Donald Trump . . . and Tupelo-born
casino headliner Elvis Presley?*

The Brats and Other Movie Stars

Vincent Price ...

and Eve Arden?

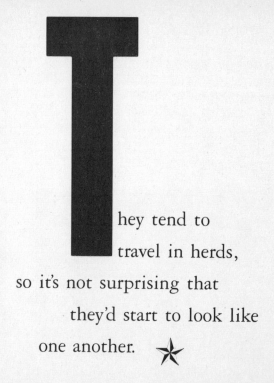

They tend to travel in herds, so it's not surprising that they'd start to look like one another. ✦

Mary Tyler Moore . . .   **and The Joker from *Batman*?**

Marie-Hélène de Rothschild . . . and Nancy Walker?

Poster-artist Erté . . .

and post-artist Lillian Gish?

Future movie footnote Patrick (*Dirty Dancing*) Swayze . . .

and current movie footnote David (*Officer and a Gentleman*) Keith?

Bruce Willis handler Demi Moore . . .

and former man Boy George?

Peggy Lee . . .

and Ginger Rogers?

**B-movie fixture
Pia Zadora . . .**

**and TV delight
Garry Shandling?**

Charlotte Rampling . . .

and Lauren Bacall?

Justine Bateman . . .

and Lauren Bacall?

Bonnie Bedelia . . .

and Mary Stuart Masterson?

Mikhail Baryshnikov . . .

and Anthony Hopkins?

Kelly (*Top Gun*) McGillis . . .

and chambermaid-heiress
Basia (Top Job) Johnson?

Cher dresser Bob Mackie . . .

and cherished actress
Jessica Tandy?

Carol Burnett progeny Carrie Hamilton . . .   **and Donald Sutherland progeny Kiefer Sutherland?**   **Sleazy-character portrayer Mickey Rourke . . .**   **and sleazy character Jerry Lee Lewis?**

Closet Canadian Hume Cronyn . . .   **and closet preppie Tom Waits?**   **Kevin Costner . . .**   **and made-for-television-version-of-Kevin-Costner Mark Harmon?**

brating the Food-Oriented

Chef Paul Prudhomme . . .

and Dom DeLuise?

Former *Laugh-In* star
Lily Tomlin . . .

and a young John Huston?

Ellen Barkin . . .

and Simone Signoret?

SPY-obsessed gossip queen
Liz Smith . . .

and Cher's daughter
Chastity Bono?

Novelist daughter of actors
Carrie Fisher . . .

and novelist daughter of
actors Patti Davis?

Actually the Same Person (Only Such Example in Book)

Dianne Wiest . . .

and Glenda Jackson?

Nancy Dussault . . .

and Bonnie Franklin?

Conductor Arturo Toscanini . . . and Kevin Kline?

Kevin Kline . . .

and John Wilkes Booth?

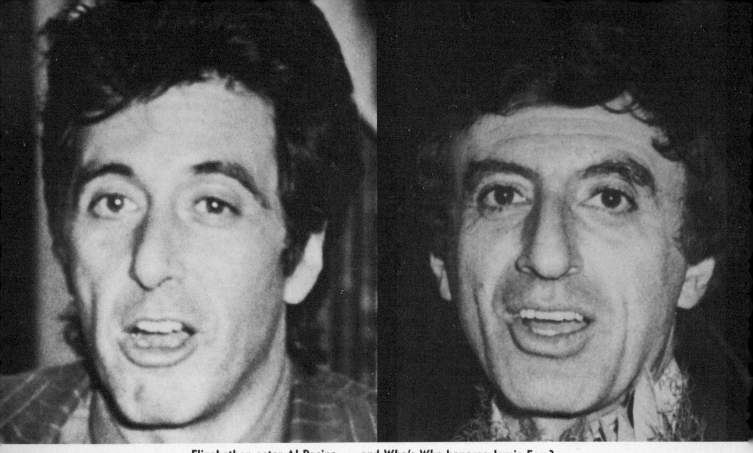

Elizabethan actor Al Pacino . . . and *Who's Who* honoree Jamie Farr?

Olivier-of-his-generation Robert De Niro . . .

and De Niro-of-his-generation Laurence Olivier?

Willem Dafoe . . .

and Chuck Connors?

Shortish *Family Ties* star Michael J. Fox . . .

and tallish tennis star Hana Mandlikova?

Meryl Streep . . .

and Mike Nichols?

The Wizard of Oz: *Open call for Dorothy at 2:30.*

The Cowardly Lion . . .

by George Shultz

For today's performance, the part of the Wicked Witch of the West will be played . . .

by Nora Ephron

The Scarecrow . . .

by I. King Jordan, president of Gallaudet University for the deaf

The winged monkey . . .   by Oliver North

Bad Sports

Shifty, aging, boyish ex-Yankee manager Billy Martin . . .

and shifty, aging, boyish actor Harry Dean Stanton?

From these seats, it could be anybody playing out there. Wimbledon champ Anthony Michael Hall returns Ivan Lendl's serve (poorly), and Harry Dean Stanton manages the Yankees. What a nightmare.

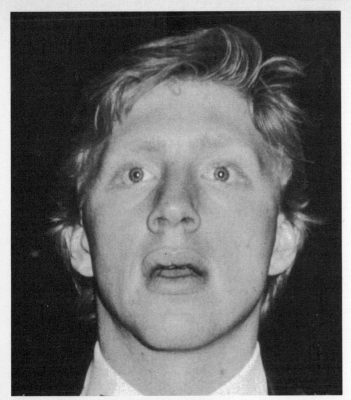

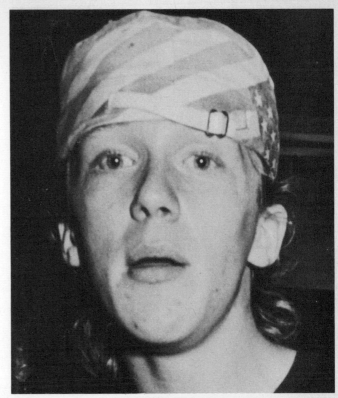

German tennis overhander Boris Becker . . .

and American movie over-the-hiller Anthony Michael Hall?

Mustachioed Mets manager Davey Johnson . . .

and mustachioed *Cheers* mailman John Ratzenberger?

Strangely self-assured skater Eric Heiden . . .

and strangely self-assured actress Amanda Plummer?

Hibbing, Minnesota-born Boston Celtic Kevin McHale . . .

and Canadian-born actor Robert Joy?

Larry Bird of the Celtics . . .

and Jon Anderson of the 70s wimp-rock group Yes?

Kansas City batsman George Brett . . .

and AT&T spokesman Cliff Robertson?

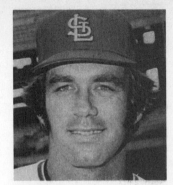

Old baseball hand Tim McCarver . . .

and News rocker Huey Lewis?

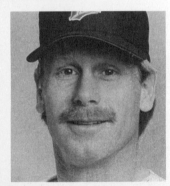

***Real* Twin Dan Gladden . . .**

and Opie-actor-turned-director-producer Ron Howard?

Phillie Von Hayes . . .

and actor Frank Langella?

Spooky child star Billy Mumy . . .

and spooky child-woman Sissy Spacek?

The World of Television

Remember the good old days before cable and satellite dishes — when TV sets had *ghosts*? Come with us now, and you'll soon be seeing double again.

And Now, the News

**Sitting in for CBS's
Charles Kuralt . . .**

**fashion designer
Christian LaCroix?**

**Sitting in for NBC's
Fred Francis . . .**

***Saturday Night Live*'s
Jon Lovitz?**

**Sitting in for NBC's
John Palmer . . .**

**former Japanese
Prime Minister
Yasuhiro Nakasone?**

**And sitting in for CBS's
Mike Wallace . . .**

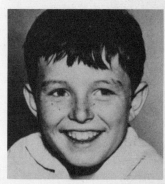

Jerry Mathers as the Beaver?

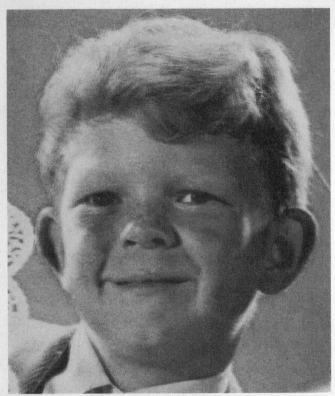

Family Affair's Jody (Johnnie Whitaker) . . .   and Mick Hucknall of Simply Red?

Sitting in for ABC's Sam Donaldson . . .

Mr. Spock?

Comedian—pizza-pitchman
Rich Hall . . .

and actor—insurance-
pitchman Buddy Ebsen?

"Separated at Birth?" buff
Jay Leno . . .

and *Life of Riley* star
William Bendix?

Former Sam Shepard costar
Chuck Yeager . . .

and former Larry Storch
costar Forrest Tucker?

The Newlywed Game's
Bob Eubanks . . .

and The Munsters'
Butch Patrick?

CBS's Walter (trusted by
1960s adults) Cronkite . . .

and Captain (trusted by
1960s children) Kangaroo?

New York nightlife star
Nell "Nell" Campbell . . .

and Leave It to Beaver star
Barbara "June" Billingsley?

Singer Sade . . .

and The Honeymooners'
Audrey Meadows?

Real Characters

F

iction, reality. We blur the
line just so that Laurence Tisch can see eye to eye
with a gang of *cartoon* dwarfs, Alexander Haig
can learn an important lesson from the
Littlest Who in Whoville, and the Dalai Lama can
befriend Pinocchio.

L.A. Law's Harry Hamlin . . .

and Sylvester P. Pussycat's Tweety?

Troublesome New York Met Darryl Strawberry . . .

and troublesome Flintstone pet Dino?

Nancy (*Hellcats of the Navy*) Reagan . . .

and Madam?

Dick (*Eight Is Enough*) Van Patten . . .

and Porky ("That's all, folks!") Pig?

Scary Alexander Haig . . .

and the scary Grinch?

Star-worshipped holy man the Dalai Lama . . .

and star wisher-uponer Jiminy Cricket?

Dwarfish CBS owner/ Diane Sawyer hanger-on Laurence Tisch . . .

and Seventh Dwarf/Snow White hanger-on Dopey?

The Cultural Crowd

You know, you *look* like a writer." Unless you're Donald Barthelme, in which case you look like a Surgeon General of the United States.

Well-marketed young author Bret Easton Ellis . . .   and well-marketed old author Richard Nixon?

**WASP monologuist
Spalding Gray . . .**

**and fake-WASP
monogrammist Ralph Lauren?**

**New York party fixture
Jay McInerny . . .**

**and TV actor Saul (*The
Equalizer*) Rubineck?**

Coffee achiever
Kurt Vonnegut, Jr. . . .

and Victor (*Highway to Heaven*) French?

Oblique fiction writer
Donald Barthelme . . .

and blunt Surgeon General
C. Everett Koop?

Congenial partygoer Norman Mailer . . .

and congenial party-crasher Robin Leach?

Seventies Revival I:

Writer Tom (*Bonfire of the Vanities*) Wolfe . . .

and comedian John (*Bizarre on Showtime*) Byner?

Seventies Revival II:

John Irving . . .

and New York Guardian Angel Curtis Sliwa?

Seventies Revival III:

Joyce Carol Oates . . .

and Shelley Duvall?

Kenneth "Mr. Theater"
Tynan . . .

and young Milton
"Mr. Television" Berle?

Gore (*Myra Breckinridge*)
Vidal . . .

and Neil (*Jazz Singer*)
Diamond?

Prodigious novelist
John Updike . . .

and litigious novelist
Renata Adler?

Southern playwright
Carson McCullers . . .

and Irish altruist
Bob Geldof?

T. S. "Tom" Eliot . . .

and neurotic-consulting-
detective-portrayer
Jeremy "Sherlock" Brett?

Living English writer Martin Amis . . .

and dead French composer Jacques Brel?

Inspired poet Joseph Brodsky . . .

and Joe Biden inspiration Neil Kinnock?

Hard-drinking, womanizing actor Richard Burton . . .

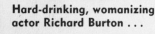

and hard-drinking, womanizing writer James Agee?

Choreographer Paul Taylor . . .

and *Star Wars'* Mark Hamill?

This mistaken-identity farce, this low, low humor we're purveying — it has no shame. Why, it can even creep into the pantheon of high art.

Conductor Lorin Maazel . . .

and Teller?

Film auteur Jean-Luc Godard . . .

and haughty film actor James Coco?

Maybe They Could Tour Together?

Carnegie Hall's Itzhak Perlman . . .

and *Hee-Haw*'s Roy Clark?

Wacky former Secretary of War Caspar Weinberger . . .

and wacky avant-garde writer-filmmaker Jean Cocteau?

Cheeseball to Cheeseball

Equally Hot by 1990

Untalented 1980s heartthrob Don Johnson . . .   **and untalented 1950s heartthrob Lex Barker?**

There's something beautiful about cheeseballs looking like cheeseballs. One is almost tempted to make sweeping generalizations.

Billy Joel . . .   **and the late criminal Roy Cohn?**

And announcing: the Fantasy Island *touring company!*

Aging but still hormonally active Linda Evans . . .

and aged but still hormonally active Ricardo Montalban

Jim ("The shame! The shame!") Bakker . . .

and Herve ("De plane! De plane!") Villechaize

New Age harp-wielder
Andreas Vollenweider . . .

and TV squat-jump
demonstrator
Richard Simmons?

Rich music-world curiosity
Barry Manilow . . .

and not-as-rich music-world
curiosity Bob Guccione, Jr.?

Love Boat's
Gavin MacLeod . . .

and Divine, who,
unfortunately, never
appeared on *Love Boat*?

Murderers' Row

Try picking one of these people out of a police lineup. It's impossible — we have a two-suspect minimum, strictly enforced.

Insufferable Brat Packer Judd Nelson . . . and Martin Luther King, Jr., assassin James Earl Ray?

Auteur—film-director Martin Scorsese . . .

and murderer-psychotic Charles Manson?

Preppie murderer Robert Chambers . . .

and preppie actress Elizabeth McGovern?

**Goldie Hawn boy-toy
Kurt Russell . . .**

**and 1950s spree-killer
Charles Starkweather?**

**Jody Foster buff
John Hinckley, Jr. . . . .**

**and J. D. Salinger buff
Mark David Chapman?**

**Superprosecutor
Rudolph Giuliani . . .**

**and would-be parolee
Sirhan Sirhan?**

Humorist Calvin Trillin . . .

and

**and nonhumorist
Lee Harvey Oswald?**

Boston Strangler
Albert DeSalvo . . .

and *Mr. Ed's* Alan Young?

Octogenarian Congressman
Claude Pepper . . .

and octo-murderer
Richard Speck?

Well-endowed gunslinger
John Dillinger . . .

and wealthy Goose-flier
Howard Hughes?

1930s socialite
Elsa Maxwell . . .

and 1930s businessman
Al Capone?

Missing Links

Widow-comedienne Joan Rivers . . . **and a baboon?**

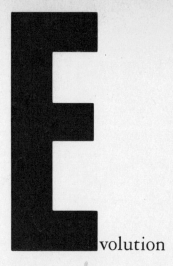

Evolution
in reverse.
The wrong
half of these
couples
has the vote.

Gorgeous lalapalooza Tammy Faye Bakker . . .   and an Ewok?

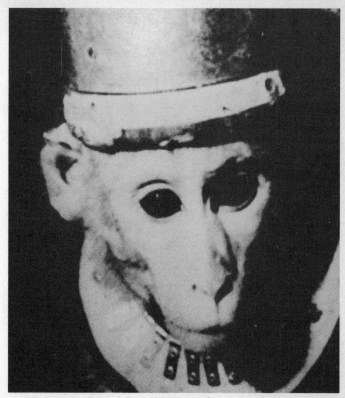

Martha Graham, the human choreographer . . .   and Yerosha, the monkey cosmonaut?

**White House pet
Dwight Eisenhower . . .**   **and a house pet chihuahua?**   **Beautiful Barbra Streisand . . .**   **and The Beast?**

**Crook—former-Vice-President
Spiro Agnew . . .**   **and a proboscis monkey?**   **Mayor-actor
Clint Eastwood . . .**   **and a primate?**

Triplets!

his is where fertility pills got us.

Edgar Rosenberg

and Ahmet Ertegun

and Allen Ginsberg

Pope Paul VI   **and Adolf Eichmann**   **and Prince Philip**

Peter Ustinov

and Philippe Starck

and Julian Schnabel

Julio Iglesias

and Francesco Scavullo

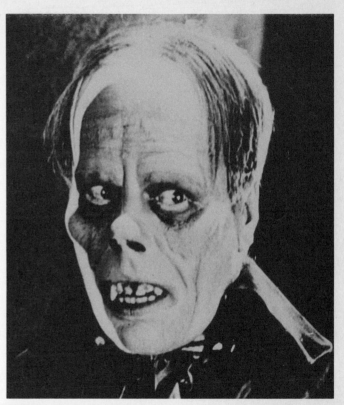

and The Phantom of the Opera

Quentin (*The Naked Civil Servant*) Crisp

and Mrs. Nelson "Happy" Rockefeller

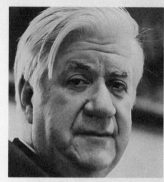

and Thomas P. "Tip" O'Neill

Economist John Kenneth Galbraith

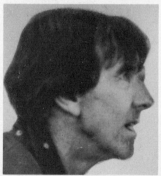

and economic actor John Wood

and economic composer John Cage

Dennis Hopper

and William Carlos Williams

and Andrew Greeley

Pallid writer Lillian Hellman

**and pal of Isherwood
W. H. Auden**

and "Paladin" Richard Boone

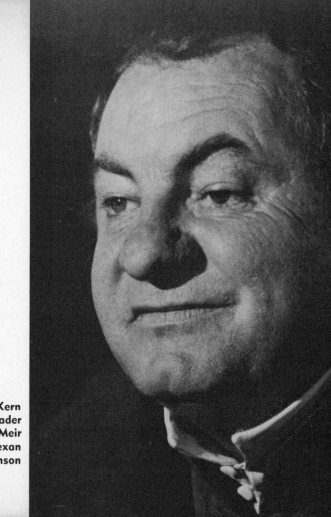

Rumpole star Leo McKern
and rumpled Israeli leader
Golda Meir
and rawboned Texan
Lyndon Baines Johnson

**Underwear pitchman
Lyle Alzado**

**and English etymologist
Samuel Johnson**

and TV jurist Raymond Burr

Female-ish male Oscar Wilde

**and male-ish female
Fran Lebowitz**

**and female *as* male
George Eliot**

PHOTO CREDITS

AN ESSENTIALLY USELESS INDEX

Erté
Ertegun, Ahmet
Eubanks, Bob
Evans, Dave
Evans, Linda
Ewell, Tom
Ewok

Farr, Jamie
Farrow, Mia
Ferguson, Sarah
Ferraro, Geraldine
Fields, Totie
Fields, W. C.
Fisher, Carrie
Fitzgerald, Ella
Forbes, Malcolm
Fox, Michael J.
Foxx, Redd
Fragonard, Jean-Honoré
Francis, Fred
Franklin, Benjamin
Franklin, Bonnie
French, Victor

Gabriel, Peter
Gagarin, Yuri
Galbraith, John Kenneth
Geldof, Bob
Gerasimov, Gennadi
Gershwin, George
Ginsberg, Allen

Gish, Lillian
Giuliani, Rudolph
Gladden, Dan
Gless, Sharon
Glover, Crispin
Godard, Jean-Luc
Goldberg, Whoopi
Gorbachev, Mikhail
Gorbachev, Raisa
Graham, Katharine
Graham, Martha
Gray, Spalding
Greeley, Andrew
Grinch, the
Gromyko, Andrei
Guccione, Bob, Jr.
Gulager, Clu

Haig, Alexander
Hall, Anthony Michael
Hall, Rich
Hamill, Mark
Hamilton, Carrie
Hamlin, Harry
Harmon, Mark
Harris, Ed
Hart, Lee
Hayden, Tom
Hayes, Von
Heiden, Eric
Hellman, Lillian
Hemsley, Sherman

Hess, Rudolf
Hinckley, John, Jr.
Hiss, Alger
Hopkins, Anthony
Hopper, Dennis
Houdini, Harry
Howard, Ron
Hucknall, Mick
Hughes, Howard
Huston, John

Iacocca, Lee
Icahn, Carl
Iglesias, Julio
Inman, Bobby Ray
Irving, John

Jackson, Glenda
Jagger, Mick
Jaruzelski, Wojciech
Jayewardene, J. R.
Jiminy Cricket
Joel, Billy
Johansen, David
Johnson, Basia
Johnson, Davey
Johnson, Don
Johnson, Lyndon Baines
Johnson, Samuel
Joker, The
Joplin, Janis
Jordan, I. King

Joy, Robert

Kangaroo, Captain
Keaton, Buster
Keith, David
Kemp, Jack
Kennedy, Edward M.
Khamenei, Hojatolislam
 Ali
Kinnock, Neil
Kirkpatrick, Jeane
Kline, Kevin
Knotts, Don
Koch, Ed
Koop, C. Everett
Kuralt, Charles

LaCroix, Christian
Langella, Frank
Lansbury, Angela
Larson, Gary
Lauren, Ralph
Lawrence, Vicki
Leach, Robin
Lebowitz, Fran
Lee, Peggy
Leisure, David
Lennon, Sean
Leno, Jay
Letterman, David
Lewis, Huey
Lewis, Jerry Lee

Lincoln, Abraham
Lovitz, Jon

Maazel, Lorin
McCartney, Paul
McCarver, Tim
McCullers, Carson
McFarlane, Robert
McGillis, Kelly
McGovern, Elizabeth
McHale, Kevin
McInerny, Jay
McKern, Leo
Mackie, Bob
MacLeod, Gavin
McMahon, Ed
McQueen, Butterfly
Madam
Mailer, Norman
Mandlikova, Hana
Manilow, Barry
Manson, Charles
Martin, Billy
Masterson, Mary Stuart
Mastroianni, Marcello
Mathers, Jerry
Maxwell, Elsa
M'Bow, Amadou Mahtar
Meadows, Audrey
Meir, Golda
Midler, Bette
Miller, Dennis

Mitchell, Martha
Mitterrand, François
Montalban, Ricardo
Moore, Demi
Moore, Mary Tyler
Morrison, Jim
Mumy, Billy

Nader, Ralph
Nakasone, Yasuhiro
Nash, Graham
Navratilova, Martina
Nelson, Judd
Nichols, Mike
Nixon, Richard
North, Oliver
North, Mrs. Oliver

Oates, Joyce Carol
Oberon, Merle
O'Boyle, William B.
O'Connor, Sandra Day
Olivier, Laurence
O'Neill, Thomas
Osbourne, Ozzy
Oswald, Lee Harvey

Pacino, Al
Palmer, John
Patrick, Butch
Pepper, Claude
Perlman, Itzhak
Perón, Eva

Phantom of the
  Opera, The
Philips, Emo
Plummer, Amanda
Polanski, Roman
Pope Paul VI
Porky Pig
Poston, Tom
Presley, Elvis
Price, Vincent
Prince Philip
Princess Stephanie
Prudhomme, Paul

Rampling, Charlotte
Ratzenberger, John
Ray, James Earl
Reagan, Nancy
Redgrave, Vanessa
Rickles, Don
Rivers, Joan
Robertson, Cliff
Robinson, Edward G.
Rockefeller, Mrs. Nelson
Rogers, Fred
Rogers, Ginger
Roosevelt, Eleanor
Rosenberg, Edgar
Roth, David Lee
Rourke, Mickey
Rubineck, Saul
Russell, Kurt

Sade
Safire, William
Sanderson, William
Sassoon, Vidal
Scavullo, Francesco
Schnabel, Julian
Scorsese, Martin
Scott, George C.
Secord, Gen. Richard
Sellers, Peter
Severinsen, Doc
Shandling, Garry
Shawn, William
Shevardnadze, Eduard
Shultz, George
Signoret, Simone
Simmons, Jean
Simmons, Richard
Sinatra, Frank
Singer, Isaac Bashevis
Sirhan, Sirhan
Slick, Grace
Sliwa, Curtis
Smith, Liz
Snider, Dee
Spacek, Sissy
Speck, Richard
Spock, Mr.
Springsteen, Bruce
Sprouse, Stephen
Stanton, Harry Dean
Starck, Philippe

Starkweather, Charles
Stern, Robert A. M.
Stiller, Jerry
Strawberry, Darryl
Streep, Meryl
Streisand, Barbra
Sutherland, Kiefer
Swayze, Patrick

Tandy, Jessica
Taylor, Paul
Teller
Thatcher, Margaret
Tisch, Laurence
Tomlin, Lily
Toscanini, Arturo
Tower, John
Trillin, Calvin
Trump, Donald
Trump, Ivana
Tucker, Forrest
Turner, Tina
Tweety Bird
Tynan, Kenneth

Ueberroth, Peter
Updike, John
Ustinov, Peter

Vagelos, Roy
Van Patten, Dick
Vega, Suzanne

Vidal, Gore
Villechaize, Herve
Vollenweider, Andreas
Vonnegut, Kurt, Jr.
Vox, Bono

Waits, Tom
Walker, Nancy
Wallace, Mike
Watts, Charlie
Weinberger, Caspar
Whitaker, Johnnie
Wiest, Dianne
Wilde, Oscar
Williams, Clarence, III
Williams, JoBeth
Williams, Robin
Williams, William Carlos
Williamson, Nicol
Wicked Witch of the
  West, The
Wolfe, Tom
Wood, John
Wood, Ron

Yeager, Chuck
Yerosha
Young, Alan
Young, Neil

Zadora, Pia
Zia ul-Haq, Mohammad